BEREAVEMENT

A collection of unsophisticated real life experiences including the full and productive pathway of a boy, then a man and now an octogenarian

John R Milne

Cover Photograph: Jonathan Milne
Design & Layout: Peysoft Publishing
Contact: johnmilne38@gmail.com
PDF/Ebook ISBN: 978-0-473-29661-9

ISBN: 978-0-473-29661-2

ISBN Bereavement - J.Milne - Peysoft Publishing
9 7 8 - 0 - 4 7 3 - 2 9 6 6 1 - 2

Paeroa
2014

For

Chris

CONTENTS

Foreword

Bereavement is a part of life that most of us will have to deal with some time. Joy and sadness, love and hate, life and death are as much a part of our lives as sunrise and sunset, summer and winter. All of life is a mystery which has provided fertile soil for poets, sages and writers since mankind discovered the art of recorded thought.

This book records various experiences and reactions of people from very different backgrounds who have enjoyed the blessings and the curses which life throws up. It also portrays these people in the ordinary and extraordinary aspects of their lives.

We cannot predict how we will respond to situations we have never experienced. One of the writers of this book, Dr. Mariette Dreyer, was used to dealing with death in her medical practice. When her children were young she used to wonder how she would cope if one of them were to die. Tragically she was destined to find out. Her story is told here exactly as it happened.

The ugly and painful reality of losing my parents at the age of seven and several more loved family members since then has done nothing to soften the blow of losing loved ones. On the contrary, it awakens memories and makes the pain more acute.

The recent death of my lovely son Chris has been extremely hard to live with. Logic and reason face an impenetrable barrier. Two things have made it possible to carry on. One is the genuine support and love of family and friends. The other is the reality of one of

Chris's favourite songs, "*There is a Redeemer Jesus God's own son*".

The pain of such a loss is not material or physical, it is spiritual. The consolation and comfort I have experienced has been spiritual. The sparkle and joy of having my boy by my side physically is no longer possible but in a spiritual sense he will always be with me. What I am trying to say is very hard to express but the beautiful old hymn, "*There is a balm in Gilead*" comes close because it is the healing power of that balm which has made the sting of death bearable for me.

The content of this book has stirred memories for the writers as they have relived their experiences. It has been said that, "Time lends enchantment to the view". Perhaps in their case it could be said, that time softens the pain because the view is not solely focussed on their death but on the larger view of their lives.

John R Milne, Paeroa, 25th October 2014

The Now Time

Written the morning after coming home to Great Barrier Island from successful surgery in Auckland for a life threatening heart condition 27th February 1998.

I am home. Kaye is home. Shalom is home. The three of us belong together. We believe a loving heart planned it that way and drew us close. Our four legged friends, Glen, Mits, Fergie, Caleb and Josh, our dog, two cats and two horses were thrown in as a bonus. On the fringe we have a big brown and white Togenberg called Shadrach. He thinks Kaye is his mum. Bottle feeding him from infancy put the question beyond doubt in his mind and I suspect in Kaye's too.

Shadrach is now a fully grown goat and of no practical use but we love him anyway. On the other hand he did manage to persuade Kaye to have me put him on page six of the Aotea Times a couple of months ago. His companions supply us with fresh milk while a disparate little group of Chooks produce a few eggs.

Not very exciting but this is our home. This is where we play out the drama and comedy of our lives. There have been other places. There has been other characters and there has been other times, but this is not yesterday, this is not tomorrow, this is now! This is where we live. This is all we have.

Lord help us to take up the challenge of this "***Now Time***"**.** Help us work with and appreciate what has been given and accept what has not. Help us be grateful and enjoy what now contains because yesterday has gone and tomorrow may never be ours. What was and will be is another world. Things are different there".

Now is a time to share. To shape and mould and create. Now is reality. Now is where we live. Now is all we have. Now is beautiful and I feel so deeply thankful for it.

John and Kaye Milne

Thoughts on Bereavements

Sometime somewhere each of us must face the reality that there is a terminus and things cannot go on as they are forever.

Denial: If you refuse to believe something is happening – such as witnessing a loved one slowly dying of cancer – then, for you, it isn't happening. This is a protective device, to guard your mind and soul from the pain, but we can never escape from reality forever. There must always be a day of reckoning.

In reading this little book you will discover actual incidents and responses resulting from that final farewell, from this life into the unknown region we call death.

A very long time ago a shepherd boy, cum poet, cum prophet, cum king, gave voice to the immortal words of Psalm 23 translated today into multitudes of languages throughout the whole world. This was the real experience of a living man called David, who looked into the face of death many times. Hounded and hunted by rivals, jealous of his outstanding looks and personality, he survived in the caves and mountains of Israel and lived to become an old man.

Though plagued by weaknesses common to mankind, he achieved greatness and immortality. The story of his life recorded in the Bible and in secular literature.

Writing on many subjects, one of the most memorable was on the subject of Death. Echoing down through the centuries over open graves his enduring words have been translated into many different languages and cultures throughout the world.

> *Yea though I walk through the valley of the shadow of death*
> *I will fear no evil*
> *For thou art with me*
> *Thy rod and thy staff they comfort me*
>
> *King David*

At the time of writing, a very dear friend Dr Hans Dreyer, a practising psychologist in South Africa, is going through the greatest test of his life. Dr Marietta, his wife, life-long companion, friend and confidante has suddenly died.
The following is an email sent early July 2014.

"Dear Hans, you have been very much in our thoughts and prayers these last two weeks. The shadow you are now under will eventually lift and be replaced by the sunshine of her great love for you. The love of your life has now gone. You have lost your very best friend and a wonderful companion who helped shape you into the man you now are. We can only imagine the pain you are going through.

"Having a foursome dinner with you and Mariette was an event. Conversation was lively and interesting. In doing so we created memories which we treasure and will always be with us. You are surrounded by caring friends and family who like us share your deep grief. Of necessity the music fades and the people melt into their own lives. You are left with your memories. Cherish these memories Hans. They are not only precious, they are irreplaceable. What you experienced with Marietta was rare in this 21st century. Yours was truly a marriage made in heaven. She is such a huge part of who you are she will always be with you.

"I wrote an article for the Hauraki Herald which thousands of people would read and have had a few calls back expressing sorrow at the passing of Marietta. She certainly made her mark and helped so many people we will never ever know so I feel good that it was put on record here in this country.

The following is the exact article as it was written and published in the Hauraki Herald:

DREYER, Doctor Marietta – We are shocked and saddened by the passing of this very lovely lady. We have lost a very precious friend. The world has lost a beautiful, caring, intelligent, generous and creative woman. The ultimate in her roles as wife, mother and doctor. Inspirational and industrious, with a strong sense of calling in her dedication to God and man, Marietta, Kaye and I have been deeply enriched by knowing you. We are privileged to be numbered among your many friends. On their behalf, we bid you farewell. It's graduation! You passed all your examinations in style. We are so grateful for the time we had together. We love you and will always cherish our friendship. You are now in God's care.

John and Kaye Milne, Paeroa.

Hans, you are still a part of our writer's group and very much in our thoughts at this time. We may not meet again but would like to keep a degree of contact with you. You have many friends here in this country, particularly Afrikaans speaking people whom I am closely associated with. They are 100% with me in what is expressed in this letter.

A memorial service was held at Te Korowai Marae. As guest speaker the following is part of what I shared. "I'm so glad we are gathering in this way to honour and reflect on the life of a very fine woman. Mariette Dreyer touched all of us in different ways.

"I saw her professionally and as a friend. Having dinner and spending an evening with Mariette and Hans was an event. It was Quality time. Together we created memories, interesting and enriching.

"They not only worked well in their marriage, they shared a lifetime of unselfish service to others.

"Hansie their lovely fourteen year old boy, the only one Mariette managed to breast feed and the apple of her eye, died in tragic circumstances.

In spite of all our resources and abilities, life throws up situations out of our control and beyond our ability to change.

"We may well ask what was it that enabled Mariette to cope and made her the woman she was? What was her inspiration and motivation? Fundamentally what was it that made her tick? Good parents? A great marriage? A privileged education? A wide circle of friends from all sectors of society? Successful children and grand children? Yes emphatically all of that! But in another sense none of it.

"Mariette's inspiration and motivation was a genuine deep sense of the spiritual and eternal. She had a very simple but profound faith in God. Jesus of Nazareth, son of Mary, a carpenter, was her hero and her God. She communicated with Him every day.

"Hans, we love you and trust God to take you through this very dark tunnel. There is something very beautiful on the other side.

In Christ, John and Kaye Milne."

John and Kaye Milne

Hans and Mariette Dreyer

Then You Did It

By Dr Mariette Dreyer

Then you did it… that one thing that we were so afraid you'd do.

It was one wintry Wednesday; a day that started like any other day…

Paulina still made you tea when you came home from school that day; you weren't feeling well, you said. Then she heard you locking our bedroom door. She even heard the safe key 'click' as it unlocked. While she stood around, wondering what on earth she should do next, Paulina heard the shot that shattered our hearts into thousands of little pieces.

Panic-stricken, she ran into the street… it was exactly the time that mothers picked up their Grade 1 and 2 kids from the Primary School over the road from our house. She ran up to the first mother she could find, hysterically clinging to her and begging her to come and help. They entered our house side by side. By this stage, blood had already begun to seep through the floorboards of the top storey.

The telephone call we received, somewhat prepared us for what was to come. "You need to come home right away. There was a shooting accident. The bedroom door is locked, and there's blood."

On the way home, Dad and I prayed that it wouldn't be serious… that you only managed to fire a shot through your arm or shoulder… that you'd still be with us.

Dad dashed up the wooden staircase and kicked our bedroom door down. I stayed in the kitchen, my eyes transfixed on the blood seeping through. There was no way someone would still be alive after losing all that blood.

There you lay on the floor, with your pillow and duvet, on the spot that you and I still huddled together in front of the heater that morning. Did you feel safe here?

It was horrific - your face, blue - and the bullet wound in your head. The entry wound on the right hand side, exactly as I'd explained to you when you casually asked me a few weeks earlier, about the temporal bone being the thinnest part of the skull. The exit wound on the left hand side was where damage was clearly evident… where the blood had gushed out.

I fell to my knees and held you; the paramedic still said, "You can leave him Ma'am, he's already brain-dead". But when I took your hand in mine, I could clearly feel a pulse - my hands instinctively moved to feel a pulse in the jugular vein. There was a strong pulse there! My precious, gorgeous 14 year old curly-haired, blue-eyed boy - my anxious cry shook the indecisiveness right out of the paramedic. "My child's heart is still beating… DO SOMETHING!!"

"Oxygen saturation of 60%", he announced after pegging the meter to your thumb. "Sixty percent is not good enough; bring a respirator, quickly!"

The policeman at the scene had one objective: to get me away from you and out of the room, at all costs. Dad calmly held me and said, "My wife's a doctor. You're not going to get her out of the room like this."

Dad's calmness helped calm me down somewhat, and I realised that I was just trying to postpone the inevitable. I realised from that first moment that your brain would have been so damaged, that it would never be able to be reconciled with what we know as "life"... it would have been foolish to keep your body alive without any chance of your brain being able to function on its own... and yet, we still decided to have you taken by ambulance to H.F. Verwoerd Hospital.

Meanwhile, news spread to our nearest and dearest. It was your big sister Hanri who had the composure to make that first call. Funny the things one remembers. I recall gasping at sips of tea through the tears - my mouth felt like cork. Where did everyone come from? They made more tea, they held us, they prayed with us and made more telephone calls...

Was it a half hour? Maybe an hour... time stood still at that stage... we decided to leave to go to the hospital. Your best friends Henno and Christo accompanied us, as did Henriette, the girl who stole your heart. Eventually three cars were packed with the friends who used to come home with you after school and a few of Dad's and my close friends.

On the way, Dad and I read each other's minds and hearts... we decided, almost with one breath, that your organs should be donated. It's funny how, prior to that moment, the whole notion of organ donation made me feel claustrophobic; when Hanri had still wanted to purchase a "Medic Alert" bracelet in order to record her organ donor status... it was as if the idea had ripened in my unconsciousness.

A pleasant, upbeat young doctor met us in the Trauma Ward and took us to you. "But Auntie Mariette, he's still breathing – look how his chest is still moving rhythmically!" Henriette got this temporary glimmer of hope in her eyes.

"No my love, it's the machine that's doing his breathing for him… he can't do it on his own any more", I explained.

I stood there with my hand on your chest, the tears crashed down mercilessly onto my blouse - your hand was still warm to the touch, just like that of any patient who was being kept alive against the odds. I think you were already in heaven, my boy; it was your body lying there - the bullet wound didn't look so horrific any more - it was covered with some gauze and plaster… looked so ordinary. We encircled your bed and Dad prayed… not that you'd carry on living, but that the Lord would give us strength and calmness.

All of us said our goodbyes; the Head of the Organ Donor Team was standing to the side, waiting to brace the topic. Fortunately we were prepared for this… the signatures were a mere formality.

At 11 o'clock that night, you were officially declared dead, with cause of death recorded as "heart failure whilst under anaesthetic."

Despite it being a time of intense pain and mourning, we were warmly wrapped in the comfort of those who cared for us.

Your pals lay around on our lawn and spoke, just like they used to, most days after school… except they were gutted… the wind had been knocked right out of them… especially young Dewan… another member of your inner circle, who only found out about the tragedy at rugby practice that afternoon.

I had always wondered what it would be like to stand at the death bed of a child… would I cry hysterically?

Would I remain in control and try and "fix" the situation?

When you and your siblings were small, I had such a fear of something happening to one of you. We were a wonderful family... Hanri aged 23, Tom aged 22, Tiaan aged 16 and you, my special one, you were only 14. What a wonderful connection we had with each other... so much so that people actually remarked on our unique bonding.

Back in the early days I prayed and asked God please to protect you children... and even though I ended my prayer with, "Lord, your will be done," I still had this underlying angst. I used to wonder what if God were to call one of you home early? Up to this point I felt I was wrestling with God about this. Until one day. And on that particular day, it was as if the Lord said to me, "My child, if it must happen, I'll give you the strength and the grace you need, to deal with it."

That peace thankfully stayed with me for years... the realisation that I couldn't look after each of you, 24/7, eventually set me free. I realised that only God could be with you all round the clock.

The day after the tragedy, our friend Judith came to us with a scripture... Genesis 15:6 "... and he believed the Lord, and He credited it to him as righteousness..."

This was a huge comfort to me. Although I knew beyond a shadow of a doubt that you had accepted Jesus as your saviour, I asked God if He would please send someone along my path, with a verse, just for me.

Then another friend came with this verse from Job 14:5: "Man's days are determined; You have decreed the number of his months and have set limits he cannot exceed…"

This was the beginning of a new perspective on your death. God established the days of your life as well. When I was pregnant with you, it was almost as if God didn't want any of my planning in the scheme of things.

While my other two pregnancies involved fertility treatment, it hadn't been so with your conception. Even though I wanted a family of four children, God did it HIS way when it came to you. You were the only little one that I was able to breastfeed and I kept thinking, "Hansie, I'm raising you for myself." The other three were nuts about their Dad and I felt I wanted one child who was nuts about me! But this was not to be! You were the one who crept even deeper in Dad's heart, my special one. You were always ready for a hug or a kiss, right up to just before that fateful day.

You were the sensitive one, especially when it came to Dad's and my feelings. You never wanted us to be sad or worried about anything. Is this why you hid your Depression so well? So that we wouldn't worry so much?

I remember when you were in Grade 7 (Standard 5 in those days)… you were so depressed and filled with anxiety that winter… you just wanted to hide away… I remember you burying your head under my arm if we were walking in a shopping mall.

When spring arrived, you seemed to feel better. Then, in Grade 8, there was the time that you fired a shot into the ceiling… the barrel of the pistol still seared your cheek…

After three weeks of treatment in the adolescent unit of a psychiatric clinic, everything went well. Yet now, in retrospect, we sadly recall little things you said, which we didn't realise at the time were pointing to the fact that that black helplessness called Depression was enfolding you yet again.

You most certainly planned the end, even though there was no note. The safe key was returned to its place; the furniture was repositioned in front of the safe... almost as if you were trying to tell us that this wasn't an impulsive decision, an accident; it was a deliberate act that you most certainly didn't want to have anyone intercept... and so you locked our bedroom door just to make sure.

Suddenly, so many puzzle pieces fell into place, with respect to the patients we've counselled for Depression. I guess we are resigned to the fact that some people, who are in such a dark place where their mood and emotional state are so disturbed that their survival instinct is destroyed and in its place an urge to self-destruct takes over. If one suicide attempt isn't successful, they try until they get it right.

Which is why we realise that suicide isn't that "unforgivable sin"... that moment when your death precedes your logistical ability to ask for a pardon... no. Suicide is the most obvious symptom of a seriously sick individual. It's the final symptom in the build-up of a disease... as impossible to prevent in some people as it is to prevent the rupture of an artery, resulting in a stroke, in other people with hypertension.

My sister Christine coined it in her note of sympathy after that terrible night. "At the end of the day, Hansie... holding his big-man cigarette, with his taut rugby physique, was just a scared, sick little boy who was standing up against this broken world, and the outrageous demands it makes on our children."

How low you must have felt… at least, now, you are finally free from that prison of despair, my boy. You're sitting with our Father in Heaven, never again to be assessed by worldly standards that only caused you pain and disillusionment. How comforting to know that you passed the most important exam on earth, with flying colours… the test of true love. Even your littlest cousin can remember your expressions of affection and your patience with the little ones!

Never again will anyone complain about your "illegible handwriting" or your hair that's half a centimetre longer than it should be, according to those school rules!

Cousin Thomas clearly recalled your conversation with him, just a few days before your death, about organ donation. Thomas said there was NO way he'd be an organ donor… that it paints the most horrific mental pictures for him… and yet you returned to this topic several times that day, stressing that "it would be cool to donate one's organs to someone who needs them!" Do you know how relieved I was when Thomas told me this?

When we heard that you had been declared dead during the anaesthesia, we were wondering whether you had died before your organs could be harvested successfully, as you had wished… but later on, a friend told us that a man in her home meeting group had been pushed into theatre at 10 p.m. that very night with kidney failure. He had undergone dialysis three times a week, and that night, your kidney saved his life, my boy! Your other kidney was donated to a man who had been waiting for a suitable donor, for 16 years.

I believe that, since the time you were born, God planned that you'd be the "match" that would save those two people's lives.

The corneas in those gorgeous blue eyes of yours were donated to a woman who was so short-sighted, she was due to receive a guide dog the following week… thanks to you, she can see today!

Even your strong, fit, healthy heart is beating in someone else's ribcage today.

These realisations left me comforted… even excited, knowing that your death wasn't in vain… your story made such an impact on certain people that it was the beginning of a whole new adventure with their Heavenly Father as well.

Rest in Peace, my boy… and know that we are at peace, because you are finally at peace.

Dinner time in South Africa

Doctor Mariette Dreyer

Dr Mariette Dreyer

Mariette was born and educated in South Africa, graduating as a doctor from the University of Pretoria Medical School in 1968.

She died suddenly on 20 June 2014.

After internship she worked in private practice from 1970 – 1980 when she became a medical doctor at the Kalie De Haas Hospital in the city of Potchefstroom. She became acting Superintendent of the Potchefstroom Hospital until returning to private practice in Pretoria in 1989, where she worked on and off ever since.

When not working there, Mariette and husband, Hans, have gratified their yearning for offshore travelling.

Between 2002 – 2008 they lived in Ireland where Mariette worked as a locum doctor. In September 2010 a long and happy association with Te Korowai in New Zealand began. She returned, as always with the love of her life, husband Dr Hans Dreyer, a psychologist on another three occasions. They regarded New Zealand as their second home, made many friends and fitted into the local community very well.

A colleague, Dr Robert Rigby writes " I want Hans and Mariette's family to know how much she will be missed by all of us, how dear she was to us and how she made our world a better place, an inspiration to us all.

What impressed me about Mariette was her grace and gentleness, her friendly disposition at all times, her professionalism and calm but serious approach to the challenges of work.

She always treated her patients with the utmost dignity and respect. I have only heard high praise for her work from colleagues and patients.

Whenever Mariette spoke of life beyond the workplace, she would always talk with such joy and pride about her tamariki and mokopuna, about her children and grandchildren.

We grieve today for someone who touched us all in a special way which we will always remember.

Mariette, goodbye, thank you for the opportunity you gave us to share some of your wonderful life, totsiens, hamba kahle, haere ra.

Robert Digby"

Why Do I Write?

It has been said ,"We spend our days as a tale that is told". A little part of that tale, or story, is written every day and read by all we come in contact with, soon to be buried or lost in fragile, flawed memory banks.

Fortunately most of us are now capable of sharing incidents and ideas independent of distance, time or memory, through the written word.

In psalm forty five, the writer enthusiastically proclaims: "my heart is overflowing with a good theme, my tongue is the pen of a skilful writer". He transforms what he is saying into writing.

Speaking and writing do the same thing. They are synonymous and yet they are different. What is the difference? One is temporal, the other is more permanent. One is reliant on memory to recall, the other is original, accurate, and accessible.

Why do I write? In the multitude of words I speak, some are more important, more meaningful and precious than others. For these reasons I want to give them a longer life and put them out of reach of distortion or manipulation with the passage of time.

Mariette Dreyer is now gone and beyond our reach. There is now no way of physically communicating with her, but the language of her heart, the core of who she was, is revealed and preserved in what she committed to writing. Reaching out beyond the boundaries of time and distance, the story of her life is preserved.

As the Patriarchal head of the Milne family in New Zealand, it may be of some interest for my descendants to know a little of where they came from and how they came to be living here.

This is a secondary reason for writing this little book.

My apprenticeship

Every journey has an end. Mine can't be very far away now. I feel very privileged to have been given eighty five very full, busy, productive and interesting years. Some marked by much pain and soul-searching, others by the joy of achievement after struggling with what seemed impossible difficulties. On reflection, the highest mountain was not in becoming a registered Secondary School Teacher after leaving school at 13, or being a Registered Master Builder in Auckland. It was in holding down a labouring job in a sawmill for two years to qualify for a five year apprenticeship in carpentry and joinery. Graduation came on my 16th birthday.

Picture if you will, winter in the north of Scotland, this 14 year old boy pushing a bike through blinding snow at below freezing 12 km to get to work. Setting out before sunrise, returning after sunset. Working a 45 hr. week, for the princely sum of $1.40. Doing a man's job for a boy's wages, day after day was not easy, but to quit was never an option.

The 27th March 1945 dawned with a nip in the air and frost on the ground. A day of great significance for me. Permanently etched into my memory. At last! An indentured apprenticeship with my very own kit of precious tools. Paid for in full by my deceased grandfather Milne. The long hard struggle to get here was over. This was the reward that made it all so very worthwhile.

Five years later at the age of 21, a qualified carpenter and joiner! Nothing seemed better than that. The arrival justified the arduous seven years it had taken to get there.

What a joy to now have the skills I so admired in craftsmen five years ago. Men who had put John Bisset and Sons on record as being one of the best building firms in Scotland. From farm gates and hen houses, to palace doors in royal residences, I felt immensely privileged to be involved in such a wide range of work with men I deeply respected. Honduras mahogany, teak, oak and many other quality timbers were used to make beautiful staircases, doors and panelled hallways. One of the highlights was to be part of a team which made 52 doors for our present Queen's ancestral home in Scotland.

I doubt very much if any of those highly skilled craftsmen who took me under their wing are alive today. Much of their expertise has died with them. We do things differently now. Education was for the privileged few. The skills and minds some of these men possessed could just as easily have flourished behind a university lectern, or on the operating table of a hospital, as they did behind a bench in that joinery shop.

These men were quite capable of being surgeons or university professors. From youngsters to old age all they ever did or aspired to do was transform rough sawn wood into works of art. It was more than a job. It gave them an identity. It was who they were. I regard my training under their tutorship to be of equal importance and value as my training at Auckland Secondary Teachers College.

That apprenticeship became the key which has opened doors to an incredible journey through a wonderful world which would have been closed and unknown.

Allow me to explain. Creating something of value, be it a piece of writing, a cake or a garden gate, gives a sense of satisfaction and purpose to the creator. In those days unemployment was high. To survive as a tradesman was not easy. These men were proud to have "Joiner", or "Carpenter, added to their name when introduced. Their name (unwritten) was on everything they made. To have created thousands of different things which has brought meaning and joy to countless people whom I shall never know, feels very satisfying. Nothing shoddy ever passed the watchful eye of the foreman. The expression "a man needs to take pride in his work" is one that we fully understood. Your name was very important in those days. What one did was connected to that. Shakespeare verbalised this beautifully when he said, "He who steals my purse steals trash, he who steals my good name steals all I possess".

The journey progressed to teacher training and a fresh new environment which was exciting and challenging. As a woodwork teacher with my own office and workshop, a vast array of tools, machinery and teaching equipment, what could be better than this? The kids seemed to love it as much as I did. Many times, driving home, I would be overwhelmed by a sense of gratitude, "am I actually being paid to do this?"

In each step of the journey there has been a sense of higher calling to do and be the best with what has been given to me. Ambition does not express what I am trying to say. It has much more to do with keeping faith with those who have gone before and honouring the energy and skills I have so freely been given. This destroyed any sense of arrogance or superiority.

Completing a project and reviewing it was like looking at a well formed rose or a magnificent tree. The raw materials came from the earth. I had no part in making them. Knowing that brings more of a sense of gratitude than pride.

Driven with the need to excel, balanced with a fear of failure, has produced energy and motivation. Everything has a time and a place. There is a time to be born and a place to be born. A time to die and a place to die. A time to plant and a place to plant. A time to build and a place to build.

In retrospect my time has passed very quickly and it has been spent in many different places. I feel immensely privileged to have seen so much and travelled so far. This is one of the things which differentiate us from our forbears.

Just as there is a time and place for everything, there is also a reason for everything. Alongside the where and when we have the why? There is a reason for doing what we do and being who we are. Often it is obscure, but whether obvious or not, it is there.

I have been described as a 'man driven'. Why? Is it pride? Selfishness? Arrogance? Ambition? I would be least qualified to answer that question. In venturing an opinion, I would say it is none of these, yet in another sense it could be all of them. We are driven by powerful forces in the sub conscious that are deeply hidden.

Self indulgence or ambition does not explain what this driving force has been. In seeking to fulfil the aspirations and dreams of others less fortunate, I have punished my body and worked long hours for no financial reward.

Invariably these experiences have brought a sense of purpose and meaning, a sharing and involvement with something much bigger than myself. What it has taught me is that it is so very much better to give than to take, but there is a time, a place and a reason for both.

It has been said, 'to whom much has been given much shall be required'. Finding the balance between giving and taking is the key to a purposeful and happy life. We shall never find very much if we are not prepared to seek. Seeking often involves moving beyond what is comfortable and familiar. But reward neutralises discomfort. The incentive to climb a mountain is in the view from the top. As mentioned earlier, the arrival was worth all the effort in getting there!

In looking back over the years there is much that I would prefer to rub out. 'But the moving finger writes and having writ moves on'. There is nothing that we can change. What is done is indelible. A truly sobering thought.

'For every action there is a reaction'. This first law of physics is not only true of the physical world. It also applies to life in general. Does this mean I may be able to manipulate the past? No it certainly does not. No action will ever obliterate a previous action. What is done will always remain set in concrete. To every problem there may not be a solution, but there is always a response.

The problem of what to do with all these negative memories remains. If they can't be erased, what can be done? In the Bible there is a story about a man called Jacob who screwed up rather badly. Years later he went back to where he went wrong and made reparations.

In taking responsibility he did not change the past, but he dramatically changed the present and future. The difficult and unpleasant action of going back created an easier more pleasant way ahead.

In retrospect, I have no regrets about confronting difficulties and hardship. From childhood I grew up with the often stated opinion, "If there is a hard way to do it Johnnie will surely find it". It was never about what was easier or more enjoyable, but what was best or right. Indecision was seldom a problem. Neither was being odd man out with a minority view. Shakespeare touched a chord deep inside of me at an early age: “This one thing above all else, to thine own self be true and it will follow as night follows day you will be false to no man”. That has not always been easy, but there has been great freedom and fulfilment in doing it.

It has been quite a trip! What then do I do with the short time left? What is important? No longer surrounded by students eager to learn, or perhaps more accurately to acquire pass marks. No more large blank sheets of paper waiting for me to draw the detail of how to put a building together. No more bare building sites waiting to be transformed into lovely dwelling places. What then is there for an old man who has lived a very full active life?

There remains two precious gifts which have not diminished with the passing years. The joy of sharing what is in my heart and the priceless gift of family.

A Little While (Rachel Joy)

That was said over twenty five years ago. It has survived all that time. It records what was in my heart, an experience, an event the way it was, authentic and original without distortion.

Much of what we say is repetitive and trivial, but some of it isn't. About three hundred years before Christ, on the other side of the world, Aristotle said something worth preserving. “We are what we do, therefore excellence is not an event, it is a habit”. A few weeks ago I was inspired by what he said because it had been put into writing. Tompkins Wake Lawyers, in Hamilton have it prominently displayed in their reception hall.

This gem, echoing down the centuries, is available to us because someone decided to put it into writing.

To pursue the question, “Why do I write?” Orphaned at seven years of age, I know very little of my parents. I have nothing that they wrote. No in depth heart to heart communication with them. There is a void there that has never been filled and never can be. I will not allow my children to carry this burden throughout their lives as I have. They will have a very clear picture of who their father was and what made him tick.

You may well ask, “Why do you write?” The answer is very simple, I write because I must.

Twenty five years ago, my very beautiful and precious baby granddaughter tragically died a cot death. Apart from being bright eyed and beautiful, she was aware and unusually responsive to her grandfather, who loved her dearly and saw her daily.

Rachel's death was intensely painful. It brought back suppressed memories of little sister Norma, and son Stephen, who had died in infancy many years previously.

Overwhelmed with grief, I reached out to God. From a broken heart, words oozed out of my mouth to my wife Kaye. Sensing the significance of these words, she put a writing pad in front of me and a pen into my hand saying, “What you have just said must be preserved.”

A Little While was scratched out on a piece of paper and smudged with tears.

A LITTLE WHILE

You came for such a little while
We wanted you to stay
You brought us treasures from a land
That’s brighter than the day

Your smile could melt an icy heart
And make it feel so gay
You taught us how to smile again
You taught us how to pray

Lord, thank you for her lovely life
Her gentle little ways
That girlie-baby-woman bit
That shone through all her days

A little while and we will see
The one for whom we mourn
A little while and we will know
Just why our little girl was born

It’s all for such a little while

But Oh the day seems long
When we can hold her once again
And sing that lovely song

Our arms are empty and they ache
Please Jesus fill this place
Repair our hearts because they break
Reveal your lovely face

Rachel Joy you brought us so much warmth, we will never be quite so cold again. See you at morning time, it's just a little while.

Chris, John, Paula, David and Norma, during happy times

Azariyia Star

My granddaughter, a small town girl called Sarah experienced a very similar tragedy. Her older sister Rachel had died before she was born so Sarah had never come face to face with death.

A little group of family and friends gathered around the graveside at Waihi in New Zealand in that Christmas season to give thanks for the brief life of Azariyia Star. We were there under very difficult circumstances to offer our love and support to Sarah. Jonathan, my son, and Sarah's uncle conducted the service.

The previous few days had been very painful for Sarah and for those who loved her. We had no answers for some of the questions those events raised.

It was Christmas time. So all around the world people were gathering to remember and honour the birth of a baby. A small town girl called Mary gave birth to that baby in a stable. Very difficult but different circumstances also surrounded that event. The baby was called Jesus.

What have these two in common? What was the reason and purpose of Azariyia's short visit? The baby Jesus softened hearts and changed lives. Azarvia has softened hearts and changed lives. Some of us will never be the same again.

Louis Armstrong's classic "What a wonderful world" says it all. "I see friends shaking hands saying 'How do you do?' They're really saying 'I love you'." The days surrounding the tragic event revealed a love and softness in the hearts and faces of all who came and went to the family home in Paeroa like never before.

Could this be the reason and purpose for our little girl's brief visit.

Grandad John, 20 December 2011.

John, Jonathan, Rhona, Chris, Heather holding Steven, Dianne and Norma

Rosita's Story

Events that laid a platform for my life were mostly sad and some were incomprehensible to me. When five months old I was given to my grandparents but my parents lived nearby. When in grade school in the Philippines I was full of hope, aspirations and dreams. I had a youthful way of thinking. Yet life was not always as rosy as I had imagined it would be.

Rosita then and Rosita Purdy today

After losing my father and grandmother, I felt the world was against me and life for me would never be the same. In mid teens I started to live alone on a small farm for about three years or more. I had my cute little farm house, cleaned the property, planted vegetables, bananas and raised livestock trying to earn money so that I could go back to school.

I was producing more than I needed until a strong typhoon caused enormous destruction. All of my livestock and all my plants were destroyed. I was so disappointed and frightened, my dreams and plans were shattered!

A month or so later, early one morning while trying to dry my rice, a cluster of coconuts fell on me. I was unconscious for hours but gained consciousness in the afternoon. I couldn't stand up so I crawled to my house.

Four days later, still very bruised, especially my shoulder, I felt loney and frightened. Nobody knew what had happened until my aunt came to visit. There was no doctor, I just boiled up some medicinal roots and herbs to drink. This remedy came to me through ancestoral skills passed on through the generations to my grandfather which I put to good use.

I was feeling better when my godfather came to ask me if I was interested in going with him to Manila. My response, "Give me a chance to think about it." After a week I decided to go. So with a paper bag of belongings I went.

On arrival at Manila I was introduced to the couple who became my foster parents. This couple opened the door which had been closed for so long in spite of all my hard work and efforts by giving me the gift of education. They opened that door. They accepted me as family and I was with them for more than ten years.

They were the ones who encouraged me and gave me moral support. They said: "One day you will decide to have your own family"

Coming to New Zealand was a very risky thing to do. I left my country and all that was familiar and dear to me, penniless, to meet a stranger in a foreign country. Yet my biggest fear was rejection! Seeking divine guidance I prayed that I wouldn't get into a mess.

My experimental marriage was a father daughter relationship because I was a Papa's Girl, looking for a father figure.

In spite of minor differences we did well in our marriage right to the very end although there were some things that we never agreed about, that is natural.

Life is not easy because there is the odd thing that still gets me down but over all I feel content with my life. God has been good to me and brought me safely this far. Thank you Lord!!

Rosita and Rex

Twenty years of being together does not seem enough for a wonderful relationship. I am blessed to have had a fine husband, step children, grandchildren, mother-in-law, family and friends.

Our relationship was based on the "Golden Rule" so it wasn't complicated. Do unto others what you would want them to do to you. For me love is understanding, sharing, forgiving, patience and devotion. There is consideration, contentment, satisfaction and sensitivity. With those qualities, joy, hope and inspiration grow. We only aspired for simple things which were within our means the bonus became evident in the form of helping hands and support from the family. Little things mean a lot.

We were inseparable. We worked as a team but I always reminded him: "No grumpiness" when we were working. He was the leader and I the follower but I always had my say. Nevertheless he meant the world to me.

In 2003 he was diagnosed with cancer, that's when I started worrying continuously but encouraged him to fight. In Rex's case there was a very slim chance. It was very painful to see him suffer. I always thanked him for loving me.

I deeply express my sincere gratitude to the whole family, my Filipino friends, neighbours and to the people who helped us by their supportive gestures. Please accept my never ending gratitude to all!

Rex, I can't stop loving you!!! However, I am setting you free.

Glen

He was a magnificent Border Collie dog. The son of a famous search and rescue champion, whose exploits were known internationally. We called him Glen, a name of endearment from my Scottish childhood.

Glen arrives on Great Barrier Island

Arriving on Great Barrier Island off the plane from Auckland, this gorgeous wee puppy dog, medicated for the trip, looking rather sad and bewildered, had no idea where he was, nor that this was to be his home for the next ten years. John, Kaye, and their ten year old son Dave, would be his family for the rest of his life. One hundred and fifty acres of beautiful Island bush would be his playground.

Glen with his adopted parents

Glen had no idea what lay ahead of him, but the look in his eyes expressed more trust than fear. We would honour that trust all of his days.

Island life was simple and predictable. With a population of about a thousand there was no bus service, reticulated power, water, sewage, or tar sealed roads. The arrival of Subritzky's barge on a Tuesdays was the highlight of the week.

Locals would gather to pick up supplies from Auckland, but the main interest would be more about who was coming and going, and what, or with whom, they were coming or going with. Also there was much more than freight picked up and dropped off. Local news and gossip was a much sought after and valued commodity. Keenly traded and freely expanded.

Glen would join me in this weekly pilgrimage. Keenly watching my every move from the safety of the Ute, aware and alert to all that was going on and in a strange sort of way it felt like I was being looked after.

His loyalty was absolute, and growing day by day. Mutual respect and trust was what that loyalty grew out of. Unconsciously, it was becoming an important segment of my life. Glen was very much part of our small family, and the simple life we shared on the island.

Glen expected to be involved in all that was going on, and was with me on the land every day. He was highly intelligent, and had this uncanny understanding of what we talked about.

Doggie Heaven, was a trip to beautiful Medland Beach. If the name Medland, or beach, was spoken, Glen would get all excited and enthusiastic. Incredibly, not even a change of tone or expression could fool him. He seemed to know everything we said. His eyes and body language were so expressive, we gradually learned what he was saying too.

Much of my life has been spent teaching young people and adults. The process has gone two ways. Over the years, It would seem that I have learned more than them. There is a story in the Bible about a Prophet being rebuked by a donkey. Could it be possible that a grown man, a trained teacher, could be taught by a dog?

It was a beautiful spring morning, "how about a run out to Medland's Kaye?' The words were hardly out of my mouth when Glen was whining at the back door of the four wheel drive Ute. That settled it, we were on our way.

The nearest land mass to Medland's Ocean beach, is South America, seven thousand miles of blue water away. Sand dunes rise high above the sea, Glen's Paradise. As he alternated between having a mock fight with the waves and racing up and down the dunes, I quietly told Kaye to keep walking while I turned for home. The big question? Where would Glen go?

The image of Glen's magnificent form, silhouetted high up in the dunes, looking longingly at Kaye, and then wistfully at me, is etched into my memory. It was no contest. There was no confusion. No hesitation. Sadly, head down, he slowly made his way towards me. His body language expressing clearer than words, how he felt, as we walked back to the Ute.

With the excitement and freedom of the expansive sand dunes and beautiful ocean beach, just beginning to be enjoyed, the worst thing for Glen was to have it taken from him. Disappointment and regret was etched into the sand with his every step. Going home was the last thing on his mind when the joy of the beach was just getting under way.

His feelings could not have been any clearer, short lived elation, now great sadness. “I don't understand dad, this is so good, so enjoyable, such fun! Why are You spoiling it? But you are my Master. You love me, you know best. I must stay with you”.

Not a word was spoken as I opened the back door of the Ute. Glen hopped in, curled up the picture of misery. But those eyes, that look, powerful and persuasive, pleadingly reproachful, expressed his feelings in absolute clarity in perfect silence.

Okay back to mum!” The words had an instant effect. Like a rocket he sped back to what he wanted more than anything. Doggie Heaven, on Medland's Beach with mum and dad. His world was in order again. No need to worry, everything was fine. Strangely I felt the same. Everything was fine.

Driving home, over the hill and down into Tryphena, it gradually dawned on me that Glen had just taught me, what no other teacher could. A lesson I would remember for the rest of my life. We only have one Master, and He loves us.

It is now several years since this was written and Glen has gone to doggie heaven. Sadly, it was only after he was no longer with us that I really understood what a huge part of my life he was.

Working on the land, at home or on holiday, he was my constant companion. Our relationship was unique and quite different from any other in my life..I have lost what can never be replaced, but am thankful for the privilege of having had such a loyal, intelligent and devoted four legged friend.

Good relationships can be taken for granted but they are of more value than any thing else. They are fragile and can be broken. The deeper and stronger the bond, the greater the pain when it ends. Be it a friend, a spouse or a dog.

A Tribute to My Brother

SANDY MILNE [30.3.27 – 18.5.09]

Come with me back through the years to a time and place half a world and whole lifetime away. Stand by my side as we gather at an open, but empty grave, at Allenvale Cemetery in Aberdeen.

Two awe struck boys stand sombrely and silently. They are brothers. Nine year old Sandy Milne is holding a chord at the head of the grave, gently and tentatively he lowers the body of his father into the earth, while his seven year old brother Johnnie does the same.

The two boys are surrounded by men in dark suits and black ties who control the other chords as the coffin is slowly lowered to the bottom of the dark cold earth.

There is no female presence. No colour or femininity to soften the scene. It is dark and it is frightening. There is no outlet for the intense pain and frightening situation. Males are forbidden to cry or show any sign of weakness.

One of the mourners commented, "Of course the two boys don't understand". Quietly I told Sandy, "We did understand, It was him who didn't." For once Sandy agreed.

Tragically, the cold hand of death strikes these two little boys only months later with the demise of their little sister Norma and beloved mother Bella. Most, if not all, of the people who stood around that open grave are long since gone, but the reality was forever written into the hearts of these two little boys.

Brothers Sandy and John Milne

Sandy and brother John Milne

To understand my brother Sandy Milne one needs to understand the immensity of the pain and the enormity of the void, the emptiness of the years without parents. The unspoken fear and insecurity, the lack of guidance when it was needed most. These painful wounds left scars which deeply affected Sandy's adult life. Some were visible, most were not. Some helped and some hindered, but they all made him a better husband and father, a better provider and homemaker.

As his only brother and a very needy and inadequate one at that, I would have been totally lost without him. It has never been said before, but the truth is I loved my brother then, I love him now. He will always be with me.

Sandy bore the exact name of our father, Alexander James Tulloch Milne. At the tender age of nine he was made aware that he was the eldest son and heir of the then prominent Milne family in Aberdeen. He also assumed responsibility for keeping his less responsible mischievous little brother safe.

We shared the same bed, went to the same schools, shared the same friends, enjoyed cricket and camping expeditions in the Grampian Hills. Spent many happy hours fishing and swimming in the River Dee as the seasons permitted.

We enjoyed marvellous freedom living on Deeside. The river and its banks was our playground. Winter would allow us to sledge down its grassy slopes, make snowmen, have snow fights and at times walk or skate all the way across while water flowed underneath.

Spring would melt the snow up in the mountains and cause spectacular floods. A tragedy for some, but a wonderland of sheer delight for us ignorant kids.

All sorts of interesting things would float down the river. Hay stacks, trees, parts of buildings, sheep, cattle, fence posts and all sorts of mysterious stuff.

In spite of a non-academic environment, Sandy excelled at school and rarely came second in any exam. He was the undisputed leader of our little gang whose most serious crime was raiding a neighbour's orchard.

The front entrance of Allenvale cemetery, across the road from our house, had impressive granite pillars facing the road. We would get two large turnips, hollow out the insides and cut a small hole on top, carve our ghoulish faces with slanting eyes, light a candle inside and set them high up on top of the pillars. We would then hide in the cemetery behind these glowing fiery smoking faces making weird other-worldly noises in the darkness.

In a more superstitious era, people, mainly old ladies, would look long and hard, then flee in terror. From our juvenile perspective this was the ultimate reward for a lot of effort and creative thought.

Sandy's one passion above all else was family. Unquestionably and totally committed to their safety and welfare. He gave up a steady inside job as an engineer to brave the hazards and hardships of the North Sea, foul weather or fine. Why? Clearly it was to earn a little more money to make life more comfortable for his family. His commitment and love for them was absolutely and totally unconditional.

Lena, you had the rare privilege of being the love of your husband's life. Sandy Milne never looked objectively at any other woman.

I remember your wedding day ever so clearly. It was a lovely occasion. You were absolutely beautiful Lena. Sandy was handsome, confident and as always comfortably in control. His organisation of the wedding and the lovely reception afterwards made my job as Best Man very easy.

It was a memorable day. Sandy paid for the entire event and never grudged a penny of it. Always astute in business, I'm sure he made a good deal.

We all have a different perspective of Sandy Milne. Given a very difficult path to cut his way through, he toiled tirelessly and fearlessly at what he thought was right.

His fundamental values, his intelligence, his loyalty and incredible sense of humour made him a wonderful, imaginative friend but a lethal enemy.

It is with a sense of very deep gratitude and privilege that I record these lines. I could not have been given a better brother. He looked after me in countless situations which my impetuosity and waywardness got me into.

There were times when we fought tooth and nail physically, but if anyone touched either of us, it was back to back and total all-out war.

Sandy, we stood together at that terrible open grave a very long time ago. We sat side by side in the Presbyterian Kirk in Holburn Street when World War Two was declared. We stood together in the Cathedral the day you were married. I am so sorry that I could not stand with you in that same Cathedral the day you were farewelled.

Go well dear brother, we will meet again in the morning.

John

"I am persuaded that neither death nor life, nor angels nor principalities nor powers, not things present nor things to come, nor height nor depth, nor any other created thing, shall be able to separate us from the love of God which is in Christ Jesus our Lord".

Rom. Ch. 8 v 28.

≈≈≈≈≈≈

[Written in Hamilton New Zealand two days after learning of Sandy's passing and three days after his funeral in Aberdeen].
1 June 2009

≈≈≈≈≈≈≈≈≈≈≈≈≈≈≈≈≈≈

Maximillian Kolbe 1894-1941

Father Max

In 1941 Adolph Hitler's Third Reich was in full bloom and going from strength to strength. The theories propounded in his book *Mein Kampf* (My Struggle), written in prison, were being fulfilled. Europe was conquered and under the heel of the Hun. America was neutral. Britain stood alone facing a mobile and ruthless military regime never before seen on earth. Faced with ridiculous odds, German High command expected Britain would surrender. When that did not happen, Herman Goering told Hitler that he would release his mighty Luftwaffe and bomb them into submission.

The plan failed for two reasons. Firstly they suffered tremendous losses when their bombers were met by the dedicated young men of R.A.F. Fighter command. Secondly Winston Churchill, the British Prime Minister, defiantly united the whole country with the words, "We will never surrender". His eloquent summary at this stage of the conflict is written into history. "Never before in the history of human conflict has so much been owed by so many to so few". That few, hopelessly outnumbered, flying mission after mission, suffered tremendous casualties. They were the brightest and the best, the cream of Britain's young men.

Hitler never conceded that he lost The Battle of Britain. His next move said that he did. In a strange twist of fate, in June of that year, his Panzer divisions were streaming through Russia backed by over three million well armed and disciplined troops.

Civilians being led to their death by German military

A new word and a new concept had been born. The word spelled terror and death for millions. Blitzkrieg (Lightning War). New mobility brought new tactics. Former indestructible defence lines were side stepped by fast moving vehicles. Troops were flown over and parachuted behind impregnable defence lines. As happened in Europe, advance was rapid, and victory followed victory, penetrating deep into occupied territory.

Were Germanic Aryans really the master race? Was Hitler right? Sadly most Germans believe they were and he was. His spirit enflamed and motivated a nation. Producing the most powerful and lethally effective war machine the world had ever seen. The humiliation of that railway carriage in Versailles in 1919 was wiped out when he triumphantlydrove down The Champs-Élysées and through the Arc de Triomphe in Paris.

Meanwhile Heinrich Himmler emerged, a brilliantly cunning man, filled with the same spirit which controlled Hitler, head of the elite N.A.Z.I. Guards known as the S.S., also the secret police, the Gestapo. Both units were picked on the basis of a high I.Q. Systematically trained to be one hundred per cent loyal to their Fuhrer and totally ruthless. Part of their training involved nurturing and caring for a puppy, then on command, strangle it to death in cold blood.

Hitler's concept of what he termed "The Final Solution, was given to Himmler. His brief was to organise and develop extermination camps to kill innocent Jews regardless of age, sex, or attributes. The most notorious of these camps was a complex known as Auschwitz. Here modern technology was used by Himmler to dispose of men woman and children on a scale of genocide never before seen or imagined. For most of the victims death was pronounced and carried out soon after arrival. Thinking they were going to have a shower they were gassed to death. The healthiest and strongest were worked to death as slave labour under constant surveillance of the dehumanised S.S. guards.

Many gifted and creative people went on a one way trip to Auschwitz for no other reason than being Jewish. A far lesser number went because of some abnormality, such as being a dwarf or slightly spastic. Some because of homosexuality. Others were there for befriending Jewish people.

Father Maxmillian Kolbe was a warm hearted Christian man who would help anyone, particularly the needy or lonely. Father Max was committed to block 14 in Auschwitz because of his generosity to Jews. A Catholic Priest with an inextinguishable love for God and his fellow men.

Towards the end of July 1941 the incredible happened. Someone had escaped without being sizzled in the maze of electric wire, shot by guards or devoured by dogs. The fortuitous man was from block 14.

Commandant Fritech ordered the inmates of block 14 to line up. Himmler would want a report on how he escaped, but more importantly what was done about it. One thing was certain heads had to roll. The S.S. glowered, tentively fingering their loaded weapons while Fritech, well fed and immaculately uniformed strutted and orated on the enormity of the offence. The half starved bedraggled group before him were deathly silent, numbed by the unknown but imminent announcement they anxiously awaited. It came soon enough. "One of you escaped; ten of you will die". The word had gone out, it was irrevocable. Death would be slow and painful. No water, no food in a dark dank cell.

One step forward, you, you, you, alternating down the line until ten men stood before him covered by machine gunners. Their fate was sealed. From the condemned a sob broke out, Oh God my wife and children. Suddenly the unheard of happened. One of the prisoners, without permission broke rank. Stepped forward towards the Commandant. Fritech grabbed his revolver, screaming, "Stah was ist los". What do you want? "I want to take the place of one of the condemned", replied Father Max.

"Why", asked the astounded Commandant. I am a single man and he, pointing to the weeping man has a wife and children.

Fritech totally unused to a prisoner look him in the eye and talk so calmly. But those eyes, he would be troubled by that look for the rest of his life. Such compassion in a hell hole of depravity and every form of abuse.

To break the moment of equality, man to man, He abruptly snapped out the question, “Your profession?” A priest was the clear firm reply. A moment of silence. That astounding reply was announced as unequivocally as Fritech’s death sentence. What he was saying, I am a Christian. There is another power I answer to. Another spirit to which I submit. My master gave his life for a condemned world. I want to identify with that and give my life for a condemned man.

“I agree”, rasped the Commandant and acquitted Frances Gajowniczek.

Prisoners lining up

The news spread throughout the camp to guards and prisoners alike. They were dumbfounded. It was one thing to give someone a slice of bread, or a spoonful of foul soup, But to give your life! This was incomprehensible. Yet is this not what Christians are called to do?

The ten condemned men filed past the “death wall”, where mass executions of prisoners convicted by the Gestapo took place. Behind the wall was block 13 where they would experience their death agony. Stripped completely naked, shoved into their death cell, The door slammed behind them, without food or water, they would wait their inevitable death in darkness.

Days passed slowly. One by one their voices fell silent. Bruno Borgewiec, a former prisoner who had to look after the death chambers, testified under oath to these things. No furniture, Just a bucket for human waste. The air was foul. Father Max never complained. He had a special gift for comforting everyone. Fellow prisoners were writhing in agony, begging for a drop of water, screaming and cursing in despair. Father Max would calm them down, inspiring them to persevere.

Every day Bruno would visit the cell to remove the corpses. The others were all weakly lying on the paved floor except for Father Max. He would be either standing or kneeling. He would look straight at his tormentors. They couldn’t stand it.

“Schau auf die erde, nicht auf uns!” they yelled. “Look at the ground not at us!”

On August 14th Bock the camp executioner, killed father Max with an injection of phenol poison. Not for humane reasons Block 13 was needed for other inmates.

In 1961 at a ceremony at the Vatican, Father Max was canonised. From the assembled crowd a man stepped forward and said with deep feeling, “I know this story is true, I am the man Father Maxmillian Kolbe gave his life for".

Thanks to Pompallier Diocesan Centre for some of the information in this article.

This impressive stained glass window, with his name Maximilian Kolbe radiating above the barbed wire fencing is on display in Szombathely, Hungary

The Kolbe Statue in Chizanów Poland

What Would I Give My Life For

In 1943 as a fourteen year old boy awakening to the horrors of war revealed daily by newspaper and radio reports, the reality of darkness and impending doom hung heavily around Great Britain. I faced the prospect of death with trepidation. Photographs of local, handsome, healthy young men, killed in action appeared regularly in the Aberdeen Evening Express.

Late on a bright starlight night, walking home from Youth Club through a park, with the Aurora Borealis reflecting high in the sky above Aberdeen and no one in sight or earshot, I fixed my eyes on the radiant heavens, spontaneously and passionately from the depths of my heart, words burst out loudly to the magnificent creation above….

> " I would give my life if I could see
> A world of peace, prosperity,
> No talk of war or hunger or strife,
> For this I'd gladly give my life."

There was no artificiality or sophistication in what was so clearly expressed. It was gut level reality.

Relaxing off duty

Airfield Construction Team near Port Suez

My First Communion

(Suez Canal Zone of Egypt 1952)

The first time I experienced the joy of Communion was in the Sinai Desert of Egypt surrounded by hostile Muslims.

As a member of the R.A.F. I was in Egypt on active service in 1952. I was not a church person. In fact could not be termed religious, but was invited by two young men to attend a meeting which was going to be held on the following evening.

We filed into a small room with a heavily armed guard at the door. Far away from home, in hostile territory, it was dangerous to make the twenty kilometre trip down Treaty Road to this meeting.

Never at any time on active service was our weaponry ever out of reach. Laying aside our .303 bolt action Lee Enfield rifles and ammunition, we felt vulnerable without the comfort and security of having them at hand. They were always close by. In the tent where we slept I had a bayonet under my pillow and my rifle and ammunition by my bed for nearly two years. It was a chargeable offence not to have them strapped by webbing to our bodies when outside the camp perimeter.

R.A.F. Shalufa, our home base, near Port Suez, was surrounded by barbed wire. Inside the main entrance gates were two trenches manned by machine gunners twenty four hours a day seven days a week, providing a diagonal line of cross fire in the event of a break in.

Around the camp perimeter searchlights scanned the desert all night from six metre high turrets connected by telephone to the guard room where men could be summoned and ready for action at a moment's notice. The reason for such high security, R.A.F. Shalufa was a bomb dump. We were guarding hundreds of tons of high explosive bombs. Strict discipline was essential for the security of all. Without the modifying influence of women and children, living behind barbed wire and machine guns soon loses its glamour – particularly when you are on guard duty one night in seven.

No one in that small room was without a heavy heart, but slowly, gradually tension eased as we introduced ourselves.

Morale in the camp was very low. The absolute contrast of where we came from and where we were, became more and more apparent. The difference was palpable. Warm smiles, kind words, handshakes and the love which glowed in their eyes gave expression to a much greater love in their hearts. We have no single English word which adequately describes what I felt. The Maori word 'Turangawaiwai', comes very close. A place to stand, a place where you are accepted, respected, and have dignity, but some things are beyond description. They must be experienced.

These soldiers belonged to another army. They were under the command of another King, whose shadow lay across the simple table with the bread and wine and an open Bible. These were the real Jesus people I had never met before. This is what I had been looking for all of my short life. They were real because their King is real – they were beautiful because their King is beautiful. His reality and beauty filled that room as we broke the bread and drank from the cup.

We were at peace with each other because we had made peace with God. Regardless of the hostility outside, there is a place of perfect peace and it is only found in Jesus.

Kasfareet, Egypt

Proud Dad leads Rhona to the altar

Stephen John with big sister Norma

Stephen John

John and Marlene Milne had a little three year old girl called Norma who was a delightful child, but badly wanted more family. Marlene had had surgery in a private hospital to achieve this.

Norma was named after John's beautiful little sister who tragically died of pneumonia at two years of age many winters ago in Scotland. A precious and much loved little girl, her memory never faded with the passing of these many years.

The desire to have more children was gratified with the arrival of a healthy little boy they named Stephen, after the first Christian martyr.

John's sad childhood strongly influenced the man he became. Stephen was to have all the breaks his dad never had. Stephen would be loved, fathered, protected, nurtured and educated like his father never was. A great future and a good family life lay ahead of him.

John's plans never contemplated death or anything uncontrollably bad happening to this lovely little boy who bore his name.

In the small hours of the morning a scream shattered the silence of the night! "Something is wrong with Stephen", Marlene called out.

Living in the Auckland suburb of Otahuhu, the family doctor was the father of the late Prime Minister David Lange. He lived a few houses up the road and came immediately. Dressed in dressing gown and slippers he looked at Stephen and uttered three dreadful words, "He is gone”. The words pierced John’s soul with agonising pain. No! Not death! Not again! Worse was to come.

The police had to be involved. A rather shabbily dressed man arrived with a grubby old suitcase and put beautiful little Stephen in it. He was taken away for an autopsy. John was livid, but powerless.

Cot death was the verdict.

On the day of the funeral, conducted by a Scottish friend, Alex Bain, it poured with rain. John was so thankful. It seemed the heavens were in sympathy with his pain. No one could see the tears freely streaming down this proud, strong man’s face, as he led the cortege carrying that little white box containing the remains of his beautiful first born son Stephen to an open grave.

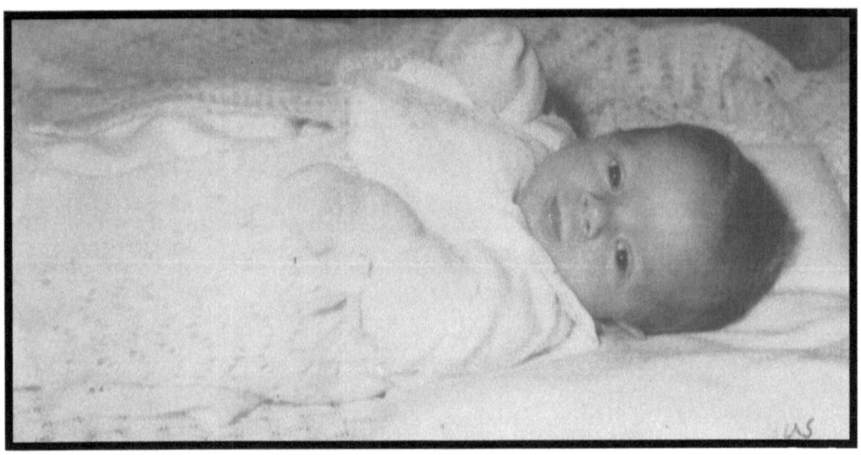

Baby Steven John Milne

ANZAC 2014

War is not glamorous so we do not glamorise it! It is ugly. It is incredibly painful and stressful. I have stood next to a mother utter the most gut wrenching wail I have ever heard. Clutching the dreaded telegram….. **KILLED IN ACTION**……

I have felt the ground shudder - the terrorising sound of bombs whistling down and wondering what it is going to feel like to be blown into a thousand pieces. Yes. War is ugly. War is horrible beyond imagination. Peace is beautiful. Peace is costly. How costly? Think about it! For many it cost them everything.

Alongside sacrifice, devotion to duty and self denial - never coming home to a loving family, or the joy of having children is what it cost. Can anyone put a price on that? This is what A.N.Z.A.C. is all about. (The unified group of Australian and New Zealand armed forces formed originally in the First World War at Gallipoli).

This is what we, here, in the comfortable safety of our homes need to remember. It is not a time for moralising, scoring points, orating or preaching. It is a time to remember, pay respect - to reflect with a deep sense of gratitude.

Some of you have fathers, uncles and grandparents who endured terrible hardship. My grandfather was a Gordon Highlander in the trenches of the First World War. My father was in the Royal Flying Corp, later R.A.F. when flight was in its infancy. While still a teenager he saw things which scarred him for life.

With no understanding of post traumatic stress then. No medication, except alcohol. He died an alcoholic at thirty seven, leaving a wife and three young children with no Welfare State to help. I became an orphan at seven years of age as a result of war. Yes, war is not glamorous.

War can bring out the worst and the best in people. I owe my life to a young officer of the 16th Independent Parachute brigade of the British army. I only met him once, very briefly. It was 1952. We were in the Suez Canal Zone of Egypt. I had volunteered to escort a truck about a hundred kilometres north of our base near Port Suez through Moslem Brotherhood country to the port of Ismailia.

It was good to get out from behind barbed wire in our camp at Shalufa, even though there was a sub machine gun on my knee and over a hundred rounds strapped to my back. What the driver and I did not know as we neared our destination was that the truck ahead of us had been ambushed and the driver and his escort killed and mutilated.

The terrorists had killed the military police on duty at the crossroads and switched the road signs round the wrong way. We were heading straight into an ambush.

The 16th Independent Parachute Brigade had literally dropped in the same morning and had just occupied the hill above the Treaty Road where we were. The young commander focussed his binoculars on the scene below and saw immediately what was going to happen to us. We were heading straight into a trap.

22 years of age, 100 per cent fit, healthy and strong, I was terrified. An icy cold shudder went up my back. My driver panicked, shaking from head to toe, the truck stalled. Suddenly, several heavily robed men came from nowhere. Not a European in sight. I slapped a magazine of ammunition into my Sten gun, released the safety catch and wound down the window with only one thought in mind. They are not going to take me alive.

At that moment the ground seemed to tremble, suddenly an elite paratrooper in full battle dress appeared. Standing in the open turret of a light tank, blazing eyes, red moustache, loaded revolver in hand, commanded my driver to reverse out of there. Obviously used to being obeyed. The driver's shuddering stopped, our truck burst into life. Inexpressible joy possessed me! With highly trained, disciplined paratroopers in lethally armed vehicles front and back, we were escorted out of a deadly predicament in style. One well aimed hand grenade would have been the end of that brave commander's life.

Not a single shot was fired. To this day I don't know the name of that young airborne commander, or what happened to him afterwards. I never got the chance to say thanks, but am forever grateful, and will never forget him.

This is what A.N.Z.A.C. means to me. That young man had no regard for his own safety or comfort. He could have lost his life. By putting our safety ahead of his own, he saved our lives. I cannot forget that. I never should forget it!

How incredible, to discovered later, if these paratroopers, regarded as shock troops and the hardest fighting force in the British army, had arrived a few minutes later, or us a few minutes earlier, they would not have been in position and you would not be reading this story.

Do we appreciate the liberty and freedom we have in our beautiful country? It is there to enjoy because our people were prepared to give it all up and lay everything on the line. What a legacy. What a heritage is ours. This is the one day in the year when we get the opportunity to remember and say thank you. Can we spare a moment, pause and reflect, rise above the trivia of here and now that surrounds us and give them our heartfelt thanks because they truly deserve it.

Chris and Jonathan's last trip on Intrepid, Tryphena Habour, Great Barrier Island

A Deathly Experience

Have you ever come face to face with the conviction that your time on earth is now over? I'm talking about an experience, not an idea, a sense that there is no alternative. This is it!

Life is fragmented into countless experiences and multitudes of ideas and feelings, most of which are either aborted or abandoned. This is essential; otherwise the mass of trivia would obliterate our thinking processes.

Strangely this magical age of computer science takes us to another level where this enormous trash bin of aborted and abandoned junk can be retrieved and reviewed with the touch of a few buttons.

We have processed and developed the spoken word, to the written word, to the recorded word. Each development has opened up larger and more complex options and strategies, and so the process continues with no foreseeable terminus.

The computer of today, with this mind boggling capability, will be strangely moronic compared with what our grandchildren will use.

Very strange things are happening all around us imperceptibly. Is it possible that there are other realities, other realms, beyond and out of reach of the here and now and our five senses? What we can see, understand and experience is constantly moving and changing. Is it possible, like the hard drive in our computer, it is still all there, but the retrieval button can elude us?

A strange and weird experience very suddenly evolved from what was perfectly normal and routine. I know where the retrieval button is, allow me bring it back up for you.

It was mid winter. Four young men, all carpenters, were in a van, returning from a job about an hour north of Aberdeen, in the north east of Scotland. It was very dark and well below freezing when it happened.

Eager to get home to a warm fire and a hot meal, the young driver had loads of confidence but very little experience. Suddenly the vehicle swerved and was totally out of control. The road cleared of snow, had a deceptive coating of thick black ice. We broadsided at high speed rolling over and over several times, then somersaulting end over end, before finally sliding on the roof, and coming to a halt upside down in a ditch on the wrong side of the road.

I was the last to crawl out of that wreck. The truly strange and awesome thing was that my feelings were very different from the other three men in that van. Full of joy, I exclaimed, “What a wonderful experience”. They, of course, thought I was brain damaged and quite mad.

Never before had I felt such indescribable elation and wonder. Propelled through this long tunnel, with the finest music I have ever heard, at full volume. There was this glorious light at the far end. If only I could reach it? Alas it was not to be! Instead, something warm and wet was running down my head and back.

Pitch dark, in the middle of nowhere, I returned to reality, with men climbing over me, the engine screaming its head off, and the wheels still spinning in the cold air. It is very unlikely any of us would have survived if they had remained in contact with the ground.

The very heavy winter coats, scarves, gloves, boots and headgear, probably saved us, also the quality steel roof of that old van.

Now, more than half a century has passed me by since then, but it is still fresh in my memory like it was only yesterday. One thing is very clear. I had absolutely no control of what took place that night, but I had absolute faith in the one who did.

NOTE: A passing motorist picked us up and took us to a roadside pub where we got cleaned up and a doctor saw us. Strangely, with such a bad accident, no one was seriously injured.

Chris and Joshua on Great Barrier Island

Stepping Stones by Chris Milne

It began with an unshakable belief that a group of people wished to visit personal harm on me. My illness developed further with audible and visual hallucinations. Typical hallmarks of schizophrenia.

Under a Compulsory Treatment Order, when 20 years old, I was admitted to Tokanui Hospital and forced to abandon my business degree at Waikato University, New Zealand. Prescribed a number of drugs, including haloperidol, risperidone and stelazine all of which I did not respond to. For nearly three months I was psychotic and delusional.

Then one day the voices departed and I started to feel better. I attribute recovery to my conversion to the Christian faith. However, others reserve the glory of my recovery to medication.

Good mental health stems from a variety of factors such as: a good relationship with God, regular exercise, abstinence from substance abuse, a healthy diet, a social life, a fulfilling occupation and the right medication, if needed.

Recovery from mental illness is not as quick or decisive as a game of chess. It is a slow process, more like the transition from an adolescent to an adult. One can expect some setbacks and recurrence of the symptoms.

I remained on a sickness benefit over the summer but was determined not to stay there. In the New Year, I enrolled at Polytechnic, in a one year freight course. For me the shorter, more vocationally oriented course was better than the long theoretical degree which I had started earlier at university .Having had a mental illness, it is important to evaluate your ability to sustain and complete a long course or degree.

I was unable to totally disguise my illness at Polytech. On one occasion, at lunch break, a classmate asked me why I was laughing- there being no reason to laugh. She continued by asking me whether I had schizophrenia, to which I replied, “Yes”. It is important to be aware that people by observation of your behaviour can uncover your illness, whether you disclose it or not.

On completion of my course, I secured a job at a freight forwarder, panicking after only three days I quit. It wasn’t that I couldn’t do the job, it was simply that I didn’t believe I could do it. It was clearly a lack of confidence.

Then I undertook a Community Taskforce, office job I retained my benefit and received a $20 petrol allowance. My confidence increased and I gained some work experience. It was a small but important stepping stone.

While at my community taskforce job I applied for a position at another freight forwarder. I felt that the interview went well and I answered all his geographical questions correctly. I given a medical questionnaire I ticked the box for mental illness. I was later told there was no job there.

I believe I lost the job due to my medical disclosure. The truth sometimes costs. People who do not have a friend or relative with the condition only hear in the media of the horror stories of the criminally insane.

After the community taskforce job I moved to a sales job – involving steel. I didn’t know enough about the product and felt incompetent. After six weeks I was asked to leave. In the words of my employer, "It's not you. This job is not the job for you."

At work I hid my illness but at home my family saw the manifestations of my malady clearly. I would sometimes talk to myself and laugh inappropriately. It was at about this time that I developed a reaction to the drug risperidone – a few of my muscles would twitch involuntarily. This condition is rare when taking risperidone but not unheard of.

It was a blessing in disguise. I was now allowed to take olanzapine which has few side effects and is a very powerful anti psychotic. The main side effect is weight gain but that does not concern me as I exercise regularly.

The next step after the setback with the steel sales position, took me to Task Force Green at an office in a rest home. This employer was very sympathetic to my condition and readily employed people with disabilities such as mental illness.

I received a free computer from Workbridge, which I still have to help with my duties. The pay was only $100 more than my benefit but I was getting work experience, learning to be punctual and increasing my confidence. (The government pays the bulk of the wages under Task Force Green to the employer, who provides a top up. The work must be of community benefit).

After working for a year at the rest home I moved to my current job in exports, at the Airport. I receive a competitive wage and no subsidy.

Through small steps on small stones I achieved financial independence from the Government – steps from hospitalisation to a secure, well paying job at the age of 25!

Jonathan and Christopher - happy times

Chris and Dianne with Bobby called after Greyfriars Bobby a Sheppard dog who followed his master to the grave

Christopher John Milne 1975 - 2014

Our son Chris was born in 1975 and spent his first six years in Howick. His four siblings were at least ten years older but they warmly welcomed him into the family and were very affectionate towards him. He was happy and secure. His niece Dianne was a few months older and they played well together from babyhood.

Father and son, John and Chris Milne

Chris's first experience of outdoor camping

When he started school at five years of age he was the only young child willing to travel on the school bus with older children. He was quite used to them!

After his parents separated Chris moved to Mangere Bridge with his mum. Later teen age sister Rhona and his cousin Liz joined them. Chris attended local Primary and intermediate Schools and later St. Kentigern's College.

As a child he loved imaginative play and was very good with words. At his interview, for entry to St. Kents the Principal asked him why he wanted to go there? He nearly fell off his chair when Chris replied earnestly; It was so he could do sword fencing. None the less he was accepted and in the main enjoyed his five years there. He worked hard and passed his exams, doing well in History and Economics as well as soccer and fencing.

When he was seventeen Chris's mum and Brian Austin married. Chris was happy with this decision and in that year the trio went to the U.S.A. to spend some time with big sister, Rhona, husband Rob and new baby Katie.

Rob was on an exchange teacher arrangement. They not only changed Schools, they changed houses, cars and pets for a year.

Next step of the journey was Waikato University where he again worked hard at his Business Degree and achieved very good results. In the holidays he worked at Tegel Chicken and was again commended for his hard work. He was told that he was the only student welcome to work at any of their N.Z. factories in the future.

Two and a half years into a four year Degree course Chris's life changed forever when he succumbed to a serious mental illness. After hospitalisation he returned home to Auckland, deciding to abandon his University Degree. He chose to do a Technical Institute course on Freight Studies. The course was completed in spite of the personal difficulties he was experiencing.

At this time Chris came to know God in a personal way and trusted Him for life decisions. Eventually he obtained a job with Fedex. He loved his work and climbed the ladder to become a Customs Broker.

At this time he was so well he moved into his own house and bought two rental properties. Tragically, several years later when things were going so well, he made the fateful decision to be *normal* and go off his medication. Soon he became extremely unwell, resigned his job and sold his three houses.

After a period of hospitalisation and back on his medication Chris obtained work in the Freight Industry again and returned to live with mum and Brian.

Selling his property meant he could buy his beloved yacht *Intrepid*. The boat was a kind of private refuge. It was in *Intrepid* where he spent his most happy days improving sails, engine, navigation and every other part, best of all going on long summer cruises and fishing trips with his brother Jonathan. It is comforting to know that they weathered foul weather and fine on *Intrepid*, enjoying the challenges of the ocean they were both drawn to and loved. Not surprising as their genetics come down from Ralph the Rover an infamous Scottish sea faring pirate in the Arctic Ocean

Since being a small boy Chris set clear goals, intently focused on them and achieved what he intended. Sadly schizophrenia polluted and invaded a beautiful mind, a good looking strong body and a man of great integrity.

What went so badly wrong in the last hours of my son's life? The ongoing challenge of coping with mental illness was compounded by a serious bout of flu. He should never have gone to work that day. Who knows what nightmare Chris experienced that night when he came home after working late.

My precious boy was found next morning by his mother, in the garage hanging from the roof.

The void, the pain, the helplessness, the regrets we feel are so intense it goes off the scale and there is no way we can even remotely describe it. I take comfort in one of Chris's favourite songs which expresses so clearly what he so passionately believed---- “There is a Redeemer Jesus God’s own Son”. I’m sure Chris got that right and he is in His care right now. The nightmare is now over son. You are beyond the reach of all that is malicious or harmful.

My boy Chris was a precious gift given to us from God. We will never stop loving you son.

Norma, Jonathan, John,
Heather, Rhona and Rob, Chris and Joy

My boy Chris

My Son Chris

Memorial Service 2 September, 2014

Thank you all for gathering with us in this time of deep sadness. Your presence and empathy is very much appreciated as we try to come to terms with our great loss. Our words, our language, are totally incapable of expressing the pain and emptiness we now feel. There are no words and there is no language that can do that.

Last week I thought I had completed a small book on the subject of Bereavement. It never occurred to me that the most painful vital chapter would be experienced and written in these last few days.

There is so much that we should have said to Chris that was never said. We had no idea that his time with us was to be so short. Forgive us son. We will try to say some of these things now in the presence of your friends and family.

Your arrival into this world was a long time coming. We eagerly awaited your appearance and had everything ready for your home coming. In spite of our carefully laid plans, specialist care, private hospital and the best of doctors, your birth, like your life, was a very difficult one.

Eventually, in the small hours of the morning one of the doctors came bursting into the waiting room with the exclamation, "Mr. Milne you have a son!" A few minutes later, a very warm glow filled my whole body as I gazed on you for the first time. That glow, which you ignited Chris, has never left me. Your life was a gift and a blessing to all of us.

Chris I loved you then and I love you now, I have never stopped loving you. We are deeply sorry for this screwed up twisted world we brought you into, so very sorry that we could not protect you from its pain and nightmares. They were as real to you as your body is to us in this building. But, we will not allow these to define your manhood. Your sense of justice, your integrity, your perseverance, your honesty and work ethic, your sense of humour and your humility and faith is the Chris we love and respect.

It was the thirteenth of April nineteen ninety six, some of us here now remember that day. Chris was twenty one years of age and I baptised him in the ocean at Great Barrier Island. It was entirely his choice. He publicly committed his life to the Lord and subsequently read the whole Bible from cover to cover. On the authority of Scripture, I can confidently say; "Blessed is Chris Milne whose transgression is forgiven, whose sin is covered. Blessed is Chris Milne to whom the Lord does not impute iniquity and in whose spirit there is no Guile. (Psalm 32)

There was no deceitfulness or cunning in Chris, totally honest and trustworthy in all of his ways. He brought honour to the name he bore.

One of my most treasured memories happened about a month ago. Chris decided to leave the big city and come spend a little time with his old dad. That quality time we had on our own was precious. It deepened and strengthened the bond that has always been there. In a strange way the father son relationship was different from ever before. I gave Chris the keys of the big car and he drove us out of Paeroa down to the Gorge.

It was a lovely sunny day so we walked together over the old Ohinemuri Bridge. Half way over we paused and chatted as the river gushed and gurgled, glinted and sparkled over the rocks below us. No orchestra or Hollywood producer could replicate that unique moment we enjoyed together. It is exclusively ours and securely locked into my memory bank for ever. We conversed maturely as equals on a wide range of subjects. Chris was very much together and confident. So much so that it seemed the father son thing was reversed. Unwittingly we created a unique and precious memory.

Driving home to Paeroa, Chris's control of the car was on a par with his conversation, faultless. Surprisingly a police officer stopped us. It was from then on that our roles really were reversed. Chris wound the window down and looked the officer in the eye, answering clearly, respectfully and logically all of his questions.

To my horror the car registration was over a month out of date. An omission Chris could never make (thanks to his mum's genes). Now the roles really were reversed. I was the naughty little boy in the passenger seat while big boy Chris took complete control and responsibility. I had never seen Chris so fluent and calm in such a compromised situation as I had placed him in. His competence and composure was in complete contrast to the feeble and embarrassed old man sitting silently beside him.

Armed with a whole lot of documentation from the officer, Chris drove straight to the Post Office, filled out all the forms, got me to sign my name and pay the bill, drove me home and put my world back in order without a hint of stress or anxiety. On the contrary, the warmth of our riverside walk continued through varied circumstances all of that day. That entire episode revealed a competence and maturity in Chris that I had been quite unaware of. The father son relationship reached full maturity, untainted and uninhibited by any sense of inequality or negative behaviour. The bonding which started at birth was beyond the influence of circumstances.

We are broken hearted at your premature departure Chris. Only now, when it is too late do we have any idea just how much we have lost and how badly waves of sickness overwhelmed you, but you will always be our Chris. You did well. We are immensely proud of you.

You survived twenty years of adult living in our hostile alien world which made ridiculous demands of you. You bravely battled on against impossible difficulties until you could take no more of it. Your decision to end it all was taken in a moment of unbearable pressure beyond the limits of our experience or understanding.

Forgive us son for not being able to stand with you in your hour of deepest need. Had we any idea of your reality we would have been there for you. Now is too late. We cannot turn the clock back and are devastated because of that. You overcame so much that we will never know. The odds were stacked so very high against you, higher than any of us understood. We are so proud of you son. You have a unique place in our hearts that will always be exclusively yours.

You leave a void in our lives that can never ever be filled. Nothing or no one can occupy that place because it belongs entirely to you.

As a boy in the north of Scotland, winters of cold snow and ice were harsh realities. Even the swift flowing River Dee would freeze over. Salmon would be frozen and trapped in pools of ice during the long, dark cold months of winter.

Miraculously they are released from their cold dark winter prison by the arrival of Spring. The earth draws life from the sun, buds blossom, birds rise in harmony to praise their creator, so eloquently expressed in Eleanor Farjeons beautiful words set to the lovely old Gaelic melody Bunnessan ;

"*Morning has broken like the first morning; Blackbird has spoken like the first bird.*"

The miracle of Spring bursts upon us with invigorating new life. The long death like winter is over. Resurrection is ours to enjoy.

Chris your winter is now over. You are out of reach of any more pain. WE LOVE YOU VERY MUCH and look forward to seeing you in a better place where there is no sorrow, tears, or parting.

You are now in good hands son, it will soon be morning.

Dad

Sailing and fishing on the Hauraki Gulf

Chris, a Brother's Tribute

Manukau Central Baptist Church, Auckland.
Tuesday 2nd September 2014

I remember the family dinner where it was announced we were expecting a baby brother. For me, as a ten-year-old enduring three older sisters the news couldn't have been more welcome, and our whole family was in a state of anticipation.

Chris was a planned and much wanted and loved member of our family even before he was born.

My memories of Chris in his early Howick years were Dad and I constructing his tree house, biking and skateboarding excursions and tenting beside rivers. I have fond memories of his milestones like first steps shared within our families lock-wood home.

It was during this time Chris first accompanied Mum, Dad and I on a newly acquired 25-foot motor- sailor, Caravel. Our life was spontaneous and fun with a kid brother at a time when adults around us shouldered all our cares and responsibilities. Chris was blessed with a Dad who was comfortable for him to try new things and make mistakes on the way.

From the age of eight and into his early teens I remember watching Chris play club soccer. He used to attend our youth group camps and was included in whatever we were doing.

Jonathan and Tania Milne

It was on one of those occasions that I took nine year old Chris to a free concert at Aotea Square in Auckland City. To my initial disappointment the very conservative friend we went with insisted we leave as Dave Dobbyn was escorted from the stage and the bottles started flying. Mum never knew just how close Chris was to being caught in the middle of the 1984 Queen Street Riot.

Chris and I were blessed with a mum in Joy who loved us and one of the expressions of that love was actively seeking out books that would capture our imagination and engage us to read and learn.

Chris read a much wider variety of books than I did. My reading was somewhat limited to series like Willard Price's, "*South Sea Whale and Diving Adventure*". I wonder how much this contributed to our behaviours later in life.

A number of years ago I spoke to Dick Park who was Chris's History teacher at St Kent's College. Mr Park told me Chris was one of the greatest successes to come out of that school. I had never seen him so animated as he stated Chris had an amazing gift of being able to express himself through the written word. Dick is having a knee replacement today or he would be here.

A few years ago quite suddenly Chris sold his rentals and purchased a 37 foot steel yacht, his beloved Intrepid. Initially we were slightly worried by this spontaneous decision and dramatic change in asset base and focus.

At the time, like many Auckland families, our life of Saturday sport, routine chores and paying the mortgage didn't allow for genuine high seas adventure. Thanks to Chris that was about to change.

Having been out of the sailing game for years and never formally trained didn't deter Chris or I. This is where I need to apologize and put in a disclaimer for Brian Austin who I'm sure was commissioned by our mum to be Intrepid's (and our) safety officer. Brian attended a Penny Whiting course with Chris and I can assure you Brian it didn't all go to waste. Those man overboard drills saved a cap on at least two occasions.

I must be honest. Initially there was some setbacks, some involving small children (my children) and rescues by the Coast Guard. But we did learn from our mistakes. We learnt that if we were rescued the money we had to donate to the Coast Guard covered not only the rescue but also our annual Coast Guard membership. We became members of the Coast Guard twice that first year.

Every year Chris and I, sometimes accompanied by others, would embark on weeklong trips out of Auckland. You wouldn't believe the sense of adventure we enjoyed. It felt like we were true pioneer explorers.

The start of these adventures was marked by blue water crossing to Port Fitzroy, The Northern Most Point of Coromandel, or Kawau Island.

Intrepid was a solid nine ton steel boat sporting an offshore rig. On more than one occasion Chris and I would just look at each other with uncontainable grins as we punched through two meter swells and twenty plus knot winds, while other yachts behind us with their sails flapping had to turn back.

Chris knew his boat intimately and worked on it tirelessly. It was his hobby and sanctuary.

I really enjoyed Chris's companionship on his boat where he was accommodating and understanding of my quirky personality traits and mannerisms. I could be myself and was accepted. Being brothers we share the same DNA, think the same and gained the same sense of refreshment and peace that comes from being immersed in the God made environment that is the ocean.

We would often exclaim there was nowhere else on earth we would rather be.

I did at times feel sad and often reflected at the end of these trips when we would be night sailing west past the lights of Auckland City, under the harbor bridge towards the West Park Marina. I was going home to a wife and family where I shared intimacy and Chris was not.

It wasn't something I spoke about and we filled our conversation with the planning and anticipation for the next trip, all the improvements we would make and how many more fish we would catch.

Over the last few years Chris has been generous with his boat and personal time spent with others on it. Some had no sea going experience, or normally have the opportunity to go sailing. He gave them a day out on the gulf that they would remember and another perspective of our City of Sails.

Chris was always patient, gentle and considerate allowing them to steer, sail and participate fully in the running of his boat. I don't know if Chris fully understood how God used him to provide pastoral care to others. I will leave you with three examples I know of in the last couple of years.

- A recent solo mum and her daughter stated her trip with Chris was her best day out, and the only fun activity they had been able to share all summer.
- A young married couple stated it was a magic day and one of the few times they had fished together and shared a common activity.
- A recently widowed man and his three boys stated, "Going out for a day with Chris was like heaven and something they all desperately needed as a family".

Well Chris, your decision last Wednesday was wrong and not consistent with how you have lived your life, but we will not allow that to define you or our shared memories.

You had a fine mind, a wide vocabulary and a big heart. Brother you don't need me to tell you that. I am confident that you are complete. You now have the last two fruit of the spirit that have eluded you in recent years. Go well dear brother, joy and peace be with you. We love you.

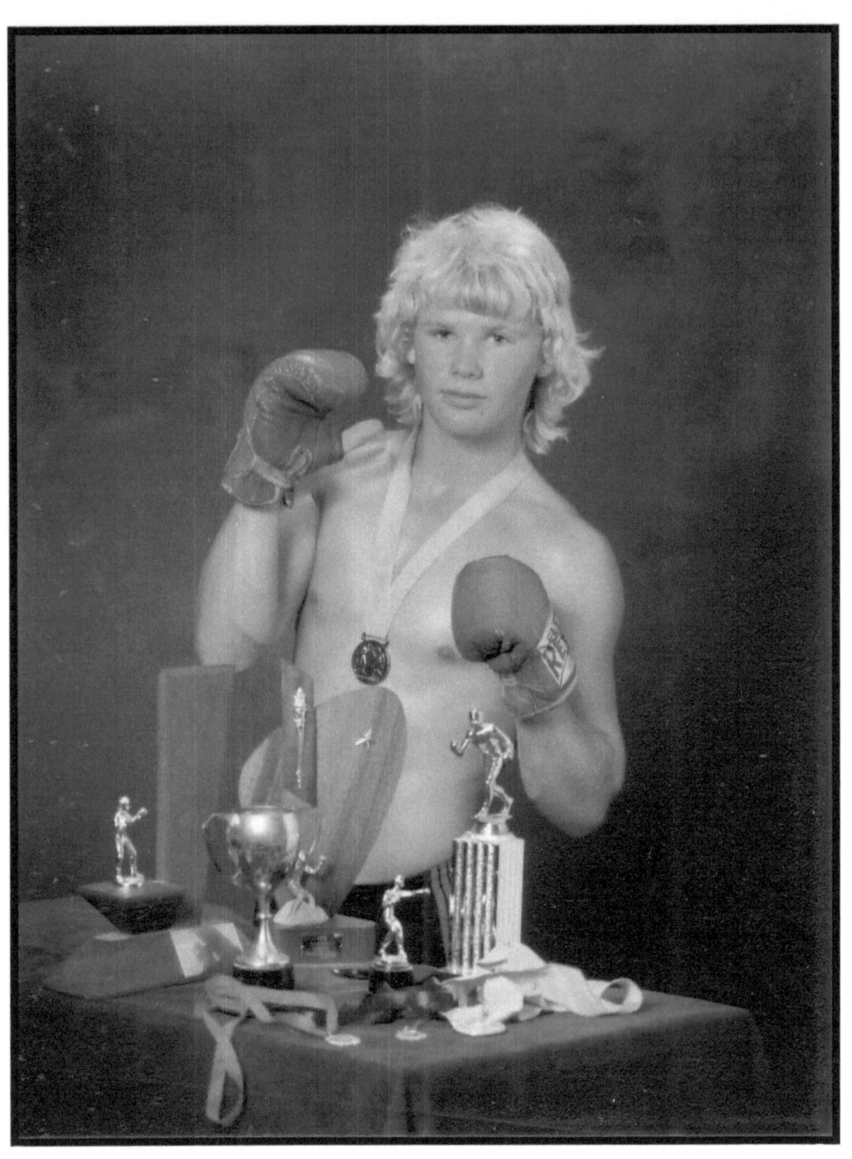

Jonathan Milne the Boxer

Robert and David, Kaye's sons, introduce Puss-in-Boots Fergie to big boy Joshua

Kaye Milne on Caleb

Kaye the midwife with Mary and baby Martha

John and Kaye

Two very disillusioned people with much failure, pain and baggage, met while seeking their way through difficult and confusing circumstances to a better more meaningful life.

Total strangers, born in two cities as far apart as any two cities could be, Invercargil and Aberdeen, their paths crossed one Sunday morning as they searched for acceptance, warmth and comfort in an Auckland suburban church. At the close of the service the minister announced that any new people were invited to the home of a member for lunch. That announcement changed the whole course of life for many people.

Thanks to the warm hospitality of a Godly middle aged couple, John and Kaye met and developed a durable friendship which exists to this day. This is how Kaye describes that first meeting and the background to it.

'Being born nine months and six days after my parents wedding date meant that I was the eldest of two brothers and two sisters. That, compounded with the reality of farmer dad's workaholic tendencies and mum's ill health, produced in me an exaggerated sense of responsibility which at times has been hard to live with.

The notion of infidelity was totally foreign and alien to my Scottish Presbyterian world view. Little did I realise that in the future I was destined to be confronted with and experience the awful meaning of that dreadful word.

Prior to that first meeting with John, life had been intolerably painful and depressing. Struggling to raise three active young children on my own and hold down a nursing job was only part of it.

While on duty in intensive care, looking after a big strong policeman just out of surgery, festooned with an array of drips and tubes he decided to go walkabout. Attempting to stop him, he twisted my body into a shape it was never meant to be in and severely damaged my back.

Surgery and excruciating pain followed. With nearest family hundreds of miles away it was a very difficult time for all of us.

Feeling lonely and despondent I called out to God with three specific requests. "Lord please get rid of this water bed and me out of the house. Lord this is a long shot, I'm lonely, could I maybe meet someone?" Amazingly the phone then rang with an invitation from an Elder of the church for the kids and I to have lunch at his place on Sunday. We go to church, meet John, arrive home and a couple are at the door to buy my troublesome waterbed. Wonderful! The first glint of light had penetrated the darkness of these last few months. All three of my requests were answered in rapid succession. Thank You Lord!

At lunch that Sunday there was this unusual larger than life man. Affable, fluent and interesting, mismatched sports socks and a blue shirt which clashed with his blue suit. Obviously single, no self respecting wife would send him out like that.

Clearly comfortable with children and noticing their confinement to the house was causing restlessness, he suggested we all take a walk. As we wended our way down to the Panmure Basin where one of John's friends had built a lovely laminated timber bridge, conversation was light and natural, but also interesting.'

The fact that John was twenty two years older than Kaye made no difference but probably enhanced the quality of their time together that afternoon. Conversation flowed freely between them from that very first meeting. Though separated by so much time and distance, they connected intellectually and emotionally from that very first day. An unusual level of integrity and openness was revealed, untainted by self interest, refreshingly different and comforting.

While it is true that our past has a bearing on our future, there is very little certainty of what tomorrow may unfold. At this time John's family of five were grown up. Apart from Christopher who had just started High School and lived with his mother Joy. Kaye's family of three were primary school age. Their father had left with another woman six years earlier and taken himself totally out of their lives. Adversity and trouble, though unwelcome, can be an incredibly good schoolmaster.

Two years later at Fowey Lodge, the home of Dr. Tony Hanne and his wife Christine, old friends of John, they were married. Another doctor friend, Ivan Howie, an ex minister, conducted the wedding. Ivan had a Medical Practice on Great Barrier Island where John owned property. The agreement was that John would father Kaye's three children and Kaye would take on John's Island home and lifestyle.

The transition to Barrier life was very hard for Kaye. No tar sealed roads, no reticulated water, power or sewage, no proper telephone or television coverage, but hardest of all was the isolation from friends and family on the mainland. In spite of these difficulties there was lots of work to do on the hundred and fifty acres. The first job was to get rid of a large colony of rats who had taken up residence in the old homestead while John was living in Auckland.

Previously In the mid eighties, John was in full flight indulging his passion for designing and building quality homes. A holiday on Great Barrier had presented an irresistible challenge to his creative instincts. Beautiful, seascape and harbour views from elevated rolling hills, Rimu, Kauri, Pohutakawa, Totara, were all there. A largely unspoiled natural part of what New Zealand once was.

A large blank sheet of paper on a drawing board had always stimulated his creative energies in the past. This was beyond any of that. The land had to be treated with the utmost respect. The footprint had to be moulded into the landscape so as not to intrude, but if possible to enhance it.

Bringing one of the first Traxcavators on the island may seem a contradiction to all of that, but heavy earth moving machinery can be used to beautify as well as desecrate the earth.

Hundreds of trees were planted to soften the roads which had to be built. They were essential in accessing the property. It was long days and hard work for John and Kaye but after five years they decided it was time to have their honeymoon.

It was the trip of a lifetime, a nostalgic look around their roots in Scotland. Kaye's paternal name of McLean came from the Island of Mull and Edinburgh. Culloden and Glencoe were part of the six week tour, but first a breathing spell in Hawaii.

After Hawaii a few days were spent in Los Angeles before flying the Polar route and down over Scotland to

Heathrow in London. This was an exciting first for Kaye, as was the trip up north to Aberdeen where the Milne roots go deep and the name is well known.

The obligatory visit to Allenvale Cemetry with John's brother Sandy and his wife Lena was deeply moving as the memory of two bewildered and troubled little boys came alive from a lifetime ago. Not a word was spoken. Tears which could not be suppressed, eloquently expressed what the years could never wipe out, the pain and loss of a family destroyed and desecrated by death.

The plan was to spend a few days with John's sister and her family in London, then on to Niagra Falls and New York, finishing with a Pacific Island hopping leisurely return to Auckland. All of that was abruptly changed on arriving at John's sister, Betty's house in London.

They learned that Chris had to abandon a very promising University course and was in intensive care with a severe mental condition. This devastating turn of events changed everything. They had been away a month but felt they could not stay away another minute longer. There was no way they could have two more weeks on holiday with Chris so ill and lonely.

John recalls:

Cancelling Hotel and Airline bookings, we flew straight back to New Zealand. Seeing Chris in intensive care in Tokanui Hospital justified all the expense and inconvenience of being with him.

Grasping firmly his ice cold hands I looked into the sunken eyes and the underweight shell of my once big wide and handsome son. The pernicious work of schizophrenia had invaded a fine mind and a strong healthy body. My boy was confused, frightened and extremely lonely in a sinister alien world.

The consuming dilemma, how can I reach him? How can I help him?

The answer came as I grasped his cold hands. Do not deny or try to negate his reality of evil and malign forces bent on his destruction. Instead lead him to a force and authority above and beyond any other, yet characterised by the ultimate in love and wisdom.

"Chris, greater is He who is in you than he who is in the world. In Christ you are safe and secure. Put all of your trust in Him. He will look after you". Slowly Chris relaxed. We then managed to talk of other things without stress or anxiety

Subsequent visits revealed gradual improvement. The latest and best of medical care and medications had up to that first visit shown no improvement, but a frightening decline in Chris's condition. I believe he was right in giving God the full credit for his recovery and remarkable rehabilitation.

I believe this revitalised faith in God brought a whole new world to his feet. The latent potential, the man Chris was meant to be emerged. He describes his story in a published article called "Stepping Stones", giving all the credit to God. These were Chris's best most productive years. Living independently, holding down a responsible job at Auckland International Airport and owning three houses. We were so proud of his perseverance and the progress he had made.

Tragically, a series of events were to unfold that shattered all of his and our dreams.

Seasons of My Life

Seasons come and seasons go. Seasons develop and seasons change. Seasons are harsh and seasons are mild. Is that not also a description of people?

King Solomon said "To everything there is a season, a time for every purpose under heaven. A time to be born, and a time to die, a time to plant and a time to uproot what is planted, a time to build and a time to pull down what is built". Bear with me, indulge an old man, and listen a little while to a small fragment of his life, which is now in its closing stages.

In my childhood and adolescence, the rhythm and flow of life was very clearly defined. Everything was organised and much more black and white than today. Living was simpler. No agonising over decisions of should I or shouldn't I? Will I or won't I? Of course there were far less choices, less opportunities. Things were more predictable. Liberality was certainly not the norm. Right and wrong were clearer defined, rightly or wrongly, at a very young age.

Progression of seasons like sunrise and sunset, were relentless and unchanging. Some years were mild, others harsh, but they never failed to come around. Swiftly they came and went. Bitterly cold and unpleasant, warm and enjoyable, they keep coming. The more that passed the faster they seemed to come. Seasons in the north of Scotland were clearly defined by their differences. A cursory look at any wardrobe of clothes revealed this.

As kids, at the beginning of winter we would go to bed eagerly anticipating that snow would come while we slept.

In the morning, we would draw the curtains and whoop with delight. Miraculously the countryside was clothed in a mantle of pure white. Breathtakingly beautiful, untrodden, pristine, pure virgin snow. A brand new magical wonderland, specially designed for us kids to play in, and discharge our overcharged energy levels.

Inevitably, winter slowly releases its grip. Way beyond our understanding or control, the movement of time brings change. It seems everything is different. Buds and blossoms appear. Birds sing heartedly from hedges and treetops announcing clearly and beautifully that spring has arrived.

Movement, development and growth follow closely on the heels of new life. But Spring must give way to summer. What we walked on in winter we are now swimming and fishing in. Warm summer evenings playing cricket on the grassy banks of the River Dee till well after midnight. The sun never went down so we didn't either. What a lovely sense of freedom of breaking through into manhood and independence. Probably more to do with that than the game itself.

On the hills above, trees, look down benevolently at the transient scene below, standing there long before we were born, they nod their leafy heads in the warm gentle breeze. Seems they are saying," everything is in order. This is as it should be, we will be here long after their little game is over and they are gone".

Recently I revisited that scene. The trees were still there, and so was the grassy patch we played cricket on. The river flowed by as it had always done. The scene was just as I remembered it. The only thing passing years had changed was me. A lifetime of highs and lows, happiness and deep sorrow, satisfaction and frustration, created this old man, now raking through the embers and ashes to make some sense out of it all.

The sole survivor of that childhood game, a lifetime ago. I felt strangely possessed, overwhelmed by nostalgia so strong tears could not be suppressed. Faces and personalities of boyhood friends came clearly and powerfully before me. I could see them and feel their presence. In that moment, time evaporated. A million actions and reactions fused into a panorama, a passing parade, an ageless saga, yet strangely outside of time. An insight into something much bigger than me, a tiny fragment of what I thought was long gone, came surprisingly, and vividly back to life.

Relentlessly, seasons continue to move. Gradually the days shorten - leaves turn a golden brown and fall. There is a nip in the air. Change becomes more and more perceptible, autumn has arrived. No amount of rejection or protest will alter the reality. Prudence demands that I accept, even welcome it.

Thus the full cycle is repeated over and over again. Swiftly the years come and go, as we all must. How then do I respond to all of this? Resentful for such a short stay? I think not! We must bow to the Almighty. Give thanks from a grateful heart for being a tiny part of this magnificent and mysterious plan.

The seasons of my life were foreshadowed in childhood. Spring with its preparation, planting and early growth. Summer with its strength energy and development.

Autumn was harvest time, reaping storing and preserving. Winter, the pace slows down. Quieter living, time to reflect and enjoy what has been gathered and preserved. A season to ponder, assess and share what the years have taught. It is now my winter time, I must embrace it and be thankful.

Permeating through incredible variety and change, there is that which never changes. Details and characteristics differ, but they are controlled and managed by a few fundamental principles and laws. Love and hate! Desire and ambition! Life and death! Apart from the gift of life, the capacity to love is the greatest gift we have been given. God is love. Made in His image, we are designed to love and we malfunction if we don't.

Beyond the understandable of here, and now, we can shift our gaze outside of circumstances, fortune or misfortune, beyond trouble and heartache, to a place of peace. Somehow, somewhere, we must ultimately seek that place of acceptance and peace. As the old Scottish ballad puts it, "Rest in peace now soldier laddie, rest in peace now the battle's o'er".

The three great pillars of faith, hope and love not only support quality living, they give purpose and meaning to all that we are, and all that we shall be. Chief among these three, towering high above all else, yet accessible and available, is **love.** It can overcome the turmoil, and storms, the winds of change, which the seasons in our lives inevitably brings.

The writer at home

BEREAVEMENT
JOHN R MILNE

Finally

The contributors of this work on Bereavement have shared their deep pain and innermost thoughts so that you the reader may have a better understanding and empathy for those enduring the loss of a loved one.

To those of you going through this dark valley, our prayer is that you take comfort in the knowledge that you are not alone. There are others out there who have gone through what you are going through and are prepared to support you.

Dr. Mariette Dreyer's analytical conclusions on the tragic death of her lovely son Hansie, page 19 has helped me enormously. She speaks with the authority of lifelong dedicated service as a qualified medical doctor, but more importantly, as a mother who has had to deal with the tragedy first hand.

Everything is moving on and changing. After the darkest stormiest of nights there is always daybreak. However unlikely it may seem now, time will ease your unbearable burden.

Thanks to Mariette, I now realise that Chris's emotional state caused his natural survival instincts to be replaced by an overwhelming urge to self destruct. It had nothing to do with his home life or circumstances. It was a deadly disease which attacked his brain and ultimately destroyed him.

Those of us who loved him were totally unaware that it was this bad. We did not understand that he had a life threatening illness so were of little or no help to him. That reality has been very hard to live with and will never leave me entirely.

This ignorance resulted in powerful and debilitating feelings of guilt and remorse. These feelings are now somewhat assuaged by a deeper understanding of the issues. The very slow process of healing has begun. The alternative is to die a broken hearted bitter old man. I know Chris would not want that for his dad.

Strangely, pain can enrich and purify. Trivial problems become less important. Values are redefined. Time with loved ones becomes more precious and life itself more sacred. Nothing or no one can ever replace what we have lost in Chris. Like all of us, he was unique, but it is ordained that each of us must leave this world one day. Chris left much sooner than we wished or expected.

It may well be that we fathers should take another look at how we define manhood for our sons. Had Chris been more dependant and less stoic he would have called out for help before the end.

The boy

The Man

The Octogenarian

John Miln's full and productive life started in Aberdeen in the north of Scotland. His amazing journey involved being orphaned at seven years of age, leaving school at thirteen, becoming a fully qualified teacher at all levels of N.Z. education, except Pre-school and owning, publishing and editing a small town, not for profit, newsy magazine. He thanks four years disciplined service in the military for changing him from a boy into a man.

Alongside his love of teaching there has been a passion for buildings in the Eastern Suburbs of Auckland bear silent witness to John's expertise as a Registered Master Builder. The Milne home, subject of a feature article in The Hauraki Herald, was designed and built by John at the age of eighty one.

While it is not uncommon to make it financially, or in business, with John's background, it is very unusual to hit the high spots in education when normal school life is over at 13 years of age. With the absence of parents, World War Two bombing and rationing, this vulnerable little boy's future looked bleak indeed.

Currently he leads N.Z. Christian Writers Hauraki, a not for profit organization. They also have a traditional Biblical world view.

www.ingramcontent.com/pod-product-compliance
Ingram Content Group UK Ltd.
Pitfield, Milton Keynes, MK11 3LW, UK
UKHW041935190726
13854UKWH00004B/1608

9 780473 296612